YOUR KNOWLEDGE HAS VALUE

Sir Gawain and the Green Knight vs. Sword of the Valiant. The representation of the Green Knight in comparison

Nicole Piontek

Bibliographic information published by the German National Library:

The German National Library lists this publication in the National Bibliography; detailed bibliographic data are available on the Internet at http://dnb.dnb.de.

ISBN: 9783346577924
This book is also available as an ebook.

© GRIN Publishing GmbH
Nymphenburger Straße 86
80636 München

Print and binding: Books on Demand GmbH, Norderstedt, Germany
Printed on acid-free paper from responsible sources.

The present work has been carefully prepared. Nevertheless, authors and publishers do not incur liability for the correctness of information, notes, links and advice as well as any printing errors.

GRIN web shop: https://www.grin.com/document/1168358

Rheinische Friedrich-Wilhelms-Universität Bonn

Institut für Anglistik, Amerikanistik und Keltologie

Sir Gawain and the Green Knight vs. *Sword of the Valiant*
- The representation of the Green Knight in comparison

Term paper for

English Medieval Studies

Winter Term 2020/21

Nicole Piontek

Table of Contents

1. Introduction

The *Gawain*-Poet introduces a mysterious and magical character in his poem *Sir Gawain and the Green Knight*. The Green Knight is a dangerous and powerful character in the beginning of the plot. He sets the happenings in motion and is the reason for Gawain's journey. However, the Green Knight is uncovered to not be the main villain of the story. Therefore, there must be hints at his weakness and vulnerability throughout the plot, just as the depiction of magical elements. The same applies to the movie adaptation *Sword of the Valiant* directed by Stephen Weeks. Although Weeks' adaptation shows clear alterations to the poem, the beginning and the ending of the plots can still be compared. As for the beginning, in both versions the Green Knight enters the Arthurian court and explains his errand. Towards the end, both versions of Gawain find themselves in the Green Chapel. Thus, these two scenes are comparable. This paper aims at answering the question whether the representation of the Green Knight in the original poem corresponds to the movie *Sword of the Valiant*. Moreover, this paper is going to focus on the aspect of vulnerability and magical elements. Thus, the following questions will be answered: How is vulnerability portrayed in contrast to each other, and in how far is magic emphasized through the depiction of the Green Knight?

The first chapter is going to focus on the outer appearance of the Green Knight. Firstly, his physical appearance will be analysed, and afterwards a selection of his properties, namely his axe and the holly branch are further discussed. Both properties are present in the poem and the movie, still there are differences in the depiction and location of them. How does the different location of the properties alter the character?

Secondly, the analysis is going to focus on the atmosphere around the Green Knight. His first appearance in the court is accompanied by mystery and fear, whereas his second appearance in the Green Chapel is differently depicted. In the poem, the Green Knight does survive as well as Gawain does. On the contrary, in the movie Gawain is the only survival of the game, as he strikes the Green Knight to death. Can these different endings be explained with a different depiction of the Green Knight?

The movie *Sword of the Valiant* is highly criticized in scholarly writings. It is said that Stephen Weeks' alterations to the plot did lead to an inconsistent and unaccountable plot. Nevertheless, I am going to analyse the movie out of a neutral viewpoint and this paper is going to try to find answers to the reason of Weeks' unpopularity.

1

2. Outer appearance of the Green Knight

2.1. Physical appearance

The physical appearance of the Green Knight represents his mightiness and strength, as well as his magical elements. This chapter analysis in how far the depiction of the Green Knight's physical appearance introduces these aspects and whether they differ in the poem and in the movie adaptation. First and foremost, the Green Knight's colour is shown in both depictions. In the poem it is written that the man is "oueral enker-grene./ Ande al grayÞed in grene Þis gome and his wedes" (150 f.[1]). Here, the Green Knight is overall green including his skin. In the movie adaptation only his armour and hair are coloured in green. Furthermore, it depends on the lighting conditions to what extend the Green Knight is portrayed in bright green i.e., while the Green Knight is sitting on his horse in daylight, he is not fully in this colour but is wearing a mixture of green and brown clothes (cf. Appendix – image 1). Still, there is a green reflection on Gawain's armour in this scene (cf. 1:29:46), which hints at a technical fault rather than a conscious decision to not portray the Green Knight in a bright colour. However, both depictions include the colour and can therefore be interpreted through it.

There are many different interpretations of the colour green that differ from scholar to scholar. One is, that the greenness connects the knight to nature and him being a "vegetation-god, a life-giving spirit" (Brewer 181). This depiction can be strengthened with the depiction of the chapel, which is also surrounded by nature. Others argue that green is the colour of ancient myths and the supernatural (cf. ibid. 183). Additionally, Brewer states that green is the colour of fairies (cf. ibid.). This would link the colour to magical elements. Furthermore, green can be seen as the colour of illusion, as hunters dress themselves in green to hide from their prey (cf. ibid. 184). With the Green Knight this would be confirmed as he deceives Gawain and the Arthurian Court and thus creates an illusion. Lastly, there is a connection of green and religion. Here, Beauregard argues that the green colour opens the depiction of the Green Knight being Christ, as "green stands for 'the preservation of life through the dead season', for eternal life [...]" (Beauregard 155). The Green Knight represents this with the survival of the beheading. Furthermore, the timing of the Green Knight's arrival hints at a religious connection, as he comes at Christmastime (Beauregard 156). Also, the knight's place is called the Green

---

[1] While quoting or referring to the poem *Sir Gawain and the Green Knight* I will refer to the lines of the poem rather than the page numbers of the used edition. All these quotations and references are taken from Tolkien, J. R. R., and E. V. Gordon. *Sir Gawain and the Green Knight*. Oxford University Press, 1967.

Chapel, and as chapel is a religious term the connection to religion is strengthened (cf. Puhvel 11). Another scholar states that when the Green Knight leaves the court without his head on its proper place, he resembles the "image of the broken body of Christ." (Sharma 191) In such religious interpretations the Green Knight's mysteries are described as being divine rather than magical. Nevertheless, as there are various meanings attached to the colour green, it cannot be stated which definition fits the Green Knight best. His character appears to be just as ambivalent as his colour (cf. Brewer 190). Besides the colour, there are more aspects which offer such an ambivalent interpretation.

The poem introduces the Green Knight with the use of many descriptive adjectives such as "aghlich" (136), "sware and so þik" (138), "þe myriest" (142). These adjectives allow an ambiguous interpretation of the character, as he is on the one hand *dreadful* (cf. 136), but on the other hand *the finest* (cf. 142). The strong use of descriptive adjectives continues with the repetition of the word *clene* (cf. 154-161). Here the Green Knight's cleanness as well as his transparency is emphasized, as Mann states: "Nothing, it seems, is hidden; there is no shabby "underneath."." (Mann 209) What the adjectives offer in the poem, the sound effects do in the movie. The Green Knight's approach to the castle is introduced by magical sounding music and harsh weather (cf. Weeks 0:04:00) and climaxes at his entrance which is accompanied by a thunder and loud noises (cf. ibid. 0:05:00). Although the sound effects may be mysterious, they still create a more dramatic and evil depiction of the Green Knight. Therefore, the poem offers an ambivalent and thorough depiction of the Green Knight from beginning on, whereas the movie relies on magical and mysterious music and dramatic sound effects, which correlate with the entrance of the villain. Moreover, the physical appearance of the Green Knight is further described.

His hair and beard are prominently depicted. The poem describes it as follows:

> And þe here of his hed of his hors swete.
> Fayre fannand fax vmbefoldes his schulderes ;
> A much berd as a busk ouer his brest henges,
> þat with his hiȝlich here þat of his hed reches
> Watz euesed a vmbetorne abof his elbowes,
> þat half his armes þer-vnder were halched on þe wyse
> Of a kyngez capados þat closes his swyre (179-186)

Thus, he has a strong beard and exceptionally long and thick hair. His hair is further described as being "longe louelych lokkez" (419). The movie shows the Green Knight also with a beard and relatively long locks. Still, neither his beard nor his hair are as exceptional or as long as the poem describes them to be. The same inconsistency is visible with the depiction of his clothes.

Whereas, the poem repeatedly emphasizes the lack of armour and the cleanness of the Green Knight, *Sword of the Valiant* shows the Green Knight in full armour. One learns in the poem that the Green Knight is wearing "A strayte cote ful streȝt" (152), "A mere mantile abof" (153) and "hose of þat same" (157). Therefore, he is wearing clothes and no armour. The lack of armour is highlighted repeatedly in the poem (i.e., 203-205). He wears no armour intentionally, as he says that he has armour at home but wanted to appear peaceful during his errand at Camelot (cf. 265 ff.). On the one hand, Gawain is described as a typical hero, especially through the detailed descriptions of his armour (cf. Lacy 172), on the other hand the Green Knight contrasts him, as he is wearing none. Furthermore, he is not wearing shoes (cf. 160), but his feet are not naked as he is wearing stockings (cf. 159). Therefore, there is no bareness in his appearance. In contrast, as already mentioned, the Green Knight in the movie is fully armoured. This armour is only interrupted with a hole in his chest area where his bare skin is visible without protection (cf. Appendix – Image 2). The hole in the armour can be depicted as a weak spot, especially as this is the spot where Gawain hits the knight in the end of the movie. Thus, the Green Knight's vulnerability is made visible for the spectator. The poem does not show this kind of vulnerability in the Green Knight's physical description. Moreover, the poem emphasizes the knight's strength through his stature.

The *Gawain*-Poet repeatedly highlights the Green Knight's massive stature and his height i.e.: "Herre þen ani in þe hous by þe hede and more." (333) Therefore, he is depicted as extraordinarily tall. This is not demonstrated in the movie, as the Green Knight has the same height as most of the other men in the court. Furthermore, in the movie he is not a "borelych" (2148) man and also not "more he is þen any mon vpon myddelerde" (2100), but a man of ordinary height and stature. Hence, the poem's Green Knight appears stronger and more powerful than the movie's version. Additionally, this is emphasized with the Green Knight's eyes.

Again, mightiness and magic are portrayed in the poem, where there is nothing visible in the movie. The Green Knight's eyes are portrayed ordinarily in the movie; there is nothing exceptional about them. Unlike the movie, here the eyes are described as follows: "And runischly his rede yȝen he reled aboute" (304). The Green Knight's red eyes emphasize his strength and mightiness. In addition to the generally known associations of red being linked to "blood, cruelty, and violence" (White 251), one can add a deeper interpretation to the Green Man's eyes. There did exist numerous theories on physiognomy in the Middle Ages. Amongst them was a handbook called *Secreta Secretorum* which stated that: "If eghen be Reed, he þat hauys hem ys coraious, stalworth,

4

and mighty." (cf. White 251). Thus, in addition to the Green Knights height and massive body, his red eyes offer even more aspects that lead to the intimidation of the court. Again, this is lacking in the movie adaptation, as the Green Knight does not have red eyes here. Overall, the Green Knight's physical appearance is described more impressively compared to the portrayal in the movie. The movie's character lacks numerous aspects which depict strength and superiority. This difference continues with the depiction of the axe, as will be explained in the following chapter.

2.2.   The holly branch and the axe

While the Green Knight enters the court, he is holding an axe and a holly branch in each hand in the poem; the movie, in contrast, omits the holly branch in his hand. The effects of this difference will be analysed in this chapter. The axe is a prominent property in both the poem and the movie. In the poem it is the last property of the Green Knight that is describes. Still, it is described in much detail (cf. 208-220) and thus, its importance is stated evidently (cf. Walls 13). The axe is introduced as being "hoge and vnmete, a spetos sparÞe to expound in spelle" (208 f.), through this its danger is highlighted from beginning on. Furthermore, the sharpness of the axe is repeatedly mentioned i.e.: "As wel schepen to schere as scharp rasores" (213) and "A dene zax new dyʒt" (2223). Therefore, the power of the axe is emphasized in the beginning of the poem as well as during the second encounter with the Green Knight. In addition, the axe is considered heavy and worthy as the Green Knight says: "I schal gif hym of my gyft Þys giserne ryche, / Þis ax, Þat is heué innogh, to hondele as hym lykes." (288 f.) The axe is given as a gift to the court; therefore, it must be worthy enough to be considered a gift. Although the axe is a weapon, Beauregard argues that the axe must not be interpreted as a symbol of war, but rather as a symbol of martyrdom (cf. Beauregard 155). As described before, the Green Knight is depicted as a soft figure, not a violent or aggressive one, which is why this interpretation makes more sense than an aggressive interpretation of the axe (cf. Beauregard 155). Still, the axe represents power and agency in the poem. A similar depiction is shown in the movie adaptation.

Here, the axe's heaviness and sharpness is emphasized, as well as its magical element. Every move of the axe is accompanied by magical sound effects, such as in the scene in which he swings around the axe (cf. Weeks 0:06:40). Here, the axe appears noticeably light in his hands which lets the Green Knight appear powerful. But this demonstration of power is interrupted: While holding up the axe, he also prominently shows his bare chest (cf. Appendix – Image 1), which will later turn into his weak spot. Therefore, with power comes the knight's vulnerability. Right before this scene, the Green Knight demonstrates the sharpness of the axe which is also highlighted by a sound effect (cf. ibid. 0:06:35). Furthermore, he calls the axe heavy himself and throws it at a man in the hall (cf. ibid. 0:06:54). Nevertheless, the man can easily fetch the axe, which makes the scene bizarre. In contrast, at another point two children struggle to carry the axe (cf. ibid. 0:10:50). Overall, the axe does not look as impressive as the poem depicted it and the depiction of the axe in the movie is inconsistent and ambivalent. Moreover, there do exist two different axes in both versions of the story.

Although there do exist two axes in both the poem and the movie, there is still an ambivalence in the representation of both. In the movie, the Green Knight pulls out two axes at once in the chapel (cf. Weeks 1:31:17). There is no difference between the two axes, which is why this scene disempowers the axe, as it is nothing special anymore. In the poem there can be made a distinction of the two axes. Whereas the second axe in the poem is "clearly an agent and symbol of redemption" (Walls 16), the first is on the one hand a Christmas gift, but on the other hand the tool that sets the plot in motion. The interpretation is therefore ambiguous (cf. ibid.). In the movie, such an interpretation of the two axes can hardly be made, as the Green Knight pulls out both axes in the Chapel and one cannot distinguish them from another. Therefore, it can be regarded as two of the same kind and therefore, there is no ambivalence here. There is still another difference which alters the interpretation of the Green Knight: the holly branch.

The poem introduces the Green Knight holding the axe in one hand and a holly branch in the other (cf. 206-208). The branch is described in opposition to the axe and is thus a sign for peace: it is an "emblem of peace" (Beauregard 154). In contrast, Martin states that the holly branch stands for immortality as a holly branch lives through harsh winters and does not die (cf. Martin 312). Therefore, it can be seen as either a peaceful symbol, or a hint at the Green Knight's survival of the beheading. Blanch further argues that the holly branch and the axe symbolize the "embodiment of choice" (Blanch 25) and with it the dilemma Gawain is in (cf. ibid.). Therefore, it portrays the inner conflict Gawain is in which is the result of the Green Knight's arrival. Such an interpretation cannot be made in the movie, as he does not carry the branch in his hand.

In the movie it is pinned to his crown (cf. Weeks 0:06:06). Therefore, the contrast, as is depicted in the poem, is not visible here. There is no choice for Gawain, as there is only the axe to pick, thus there is no tension. Blanch argues that in the movie Gawain is forced to seek out the Green Knight because of the missing branch in the hands of the

Green Knight (cf. Blanch 25). Hence, the missing holly branch in the Green Knight's hand leads to the failure "to spark internal conflict within the young knight […]." (Blanch 26) Concluding, the poem depicts the Green Knight as a more ambivalent and profound character. In the movie the character is portrayed inconsistently and less powerful.

3. The atmosphere around the Green Knight

3.1. The Green Knight's first appearance

With the Green Knight's appearance come the reactions of the people in the court. These reactions are similar in the poem and the movie. In both versions the people are mostly silent and afraid. The *Gawain*-Poet describes the crowd's reaction as follows: "And al stouned at his steuen and stonstil seten / In a swoghe sylence Þurȝ Þe sale riche." (242 f.) This depiction continues after the Green Knight explains his errand: "If he hem stowned vpon fyrst, stiller were Þanne." (301) The people stay quiet throughout the whole scene, only king Arthur and his nephew Gawain dare to speak. Similar happens in the movie adaptation. Here, no one talks during the Green Knight's entrance and his speech. The people only make a sound when the Green Knight demonstrates the power of his axe, as they scream out in fear (cf. Weeks 0:07:04). Although the same silent and thus tense atmosphere is created, the movie manages to break this atmosphere when a knight makes a comment to Arthur while the Green Knight is explaining the game (cf. ibid. 0:08:05). Through this disruption of the silence, the tension is disrupted as well. Therefore, the poem's tense atmosphere appears to be stronger. Furthermore, the Green Knight's superiority is represented differently in both depictions.

In the poem, the Green Man's dominance and superiority is shown throughout the whole time he is at Camelot's court. Most prominently this is visible through his acts of insulting the court to present himself as the dominant person. For instance, the Green Knight wants to subordinate Arthur's position as a king by disrespecting him in various ways (cf. Pons-Sanz 225), like with the refusal of the dwelling which Arthur offers the knight (cf. 250 ff.). Furthermore, he laughs at Arthur when no one wants to take part in his game (cf. 309 ff.). In addition, he insults Arthur's men by saying: "Hit arn aboute on Þis bench bot berdlez chylder […] Here is no mon me to mach, fo myȝtez so wayke." (280 ff.). The Green Knight considers bearded men stronger than beardless, and as he himself has a thick beard, he calls himself stronger than the other men. Hence, through insulting Arthur and his court, he empowers himself and makes himself superior.

Sword of the Valiant is inconsistent while portraying the Green Knight. Throughout the court scene he is mostly seen through an eye-level angle or a high-angle shot. The latter is usually used to indicate that people are looking down on the subject, or it can even symbolize "weakness, passiveness, and powerlessness" (Mercado 9). However, in the scene where he is swinging the axe around and in the scenes in which he is sitting on his horse a low-angle shot is used. This emphasizes power and superiority (cf. ibid.). Through the usage of all three varieties of angles, there cannot be made a clear interpretation of the portrayal of the Green Knight. However, the strong sound effects which accompany his actions strengthen his prominence. Especially in the contrast of the silence of the crowd, music has a large effect i.e., when he explains his errand and suddenly music sets in (cf. Weeks 0:07:08). This creates an atmosphere in which the Green Knight's speech is foregrounded and therefore dominant. In addition, the beard aspect is picked up in the movie as well. He explains to Gawain that he will give him twelve months to make sure that he grows a beard and thus becomes a man (cf. ibid. 0:13:58). Therefore, he feels superior as he himself has a beard and is therefore stronger. Nevertheless, this superiority is weakened as the men in the crowd in the background all have beards (cf. ibid. 0:06:06) and are therefore considered strong men as well. Moreover, the Green Knight's courteous behaviour is emphasized.

The Green Knight behaves courteously throughout the whole scene. He does not want to fight and act violently on the holly Christmastime, but highlights that his errand is a game, not a fight (cf. Martin 312). His courteous behaviour is strengthened in the poem by a contrast. The people in the court kick away the Green Knight's head after the beheading (cf. 428) and thus react violently. This discourtesy stands in contrast to the continuous courtesy of the Green Knight (cf. ibid. 313), because even after the stroke while his head is separated from his body, he stays calm and reminds Gawain of his oath to continue the game. He is neither angry nor ashamed, or as Martin puts it: "He has totally kept his head." (ibid.) The movie contrasts this, as the Green Knight puts his head back on his body only shortly after the blow. Here the emphasize of his courteous and chivalric behaviour is lost. Moreover, the poem again strengthens the superiority of the Green Knight by stating his fame. He tells Gawain that he has to ask around to find his Green Chapel (cf. 454), thus he is known by many people. The movie in contrast, does not mention the Green Chapel or his fame. Here the Green Knight only says: "If you do not find me, I will most surely find you." (Weeks 0:15:20) Furthermore, the stroke itself highlights the different sets of vulnerability as well as the horrific scene of the beheading.

As mentioned before, the weak points of the Green Knight are differently depicted in the two versions of the story. In the poem, the Green Knight uncovers his bare neck while preparing for the stroke. This is described with the following terms: "Þe lere he discouerez" (418) and "the naked nec" (420). Furthermore, the blade cuts through "Þe schyire grece" (425) and "Þe blod brayd fro Þe body" (429). All these terms (naked neck, soft flesh, and blood) are signs of vulnerability. Hence, the Green Knight is depicted as vulnerable in this scene. Still, he survives the stroke. After his survival he is no longer described as having a "fayre hede" (427) or a "lufly hed" (433), but as a man with an "vgly bodi" (441). The change from positive to negative adjectives happens in the wheel of the stanza. Through this, the reaction of the people is emphasized, who now fear the Green Knight even more and are appalled of the unnatural happening. The movie accompanies Gawain and the blow with heroic music, which immediately creates an atmosphere of Gawain being a hero and thus empowering the Green Knight. Again, a high angle-shot creates submissiveness of the Green Knight. When the Green Knights head is cut off and lies on the ground it says: "Body, come to me, my body." (Weeks 0:12:25). This almost comedic element further disempowers the Green Knight. Nevertheless, his superiority is visible, as he bows down to take the blow. He presents his neck (though not uncovering it from is hair) and shows his allegedly vulnerable body part, while he is actually hiding his true weak point: the bare chest. Overall, the poem creates a more tense atmosphere and thus a stronger and more dominant character with the Green Knight. The movie is again inconsistent and thus difficult to analyse. Moreover, the scenes around the Green Chapel show more differences of the representation of the Green Knight.

3.2.   The Green Chapel

The last scenes around the Green Chapel emphasize the difference of the depictions of the Green Knight the most. Firstly, the poem introduces the reader to the chapel and its owner through a guide. This guide offers a description before Gawain and the reader get to know the surroundings for themselves. He says that the Green Knight is "Þe worst vpon erÞe" (2098) and that "Þer passes non bi Þat place so proude in his armes / Þat he ne dyngez hym to deÞe with dynt of his honed." (2104 f.) Therefore, he warns Gawain of the danger that he is approaching, as he will most probably lose his life to the Green Knight. The function of the guide is to increase Gawain's fear and to lead him to uncourteously behaviour by not going to the chapel (cf. Morgan 21). He does that by stating that he is worrying about Gawain's life and then describing the Green Knight as a dangerous man which corresponds Gawain's attitude towards the Green Knight (cf. ibid.). This increases the tension of the overall plot and creates suspense. As the movie does not include the guide, it is missing these attributes. Furthermore, the poem offers a more detailed description of the surroundings of the Green Chapel.

Whereas the poem describes a dangerous and simultaneously magical place, the movie only gives a glimpse of the Green Chapel. In the poem Gawain describes the surroundings of the chapel as follows: "Þis oritore is vgly, with erbez ouergrowen" (2190), it is therefore ugly and overgrown. He continues by saying: "Wel bisemez Þe wyȝe wruxled in grene" (2191). Here, he directly links the ugly place to the Green Knight and calls it fitting to his character. Hereafter follows a superstitious description of the place which is emphasized by an alliteration: "Dele here his deuocioun on Þe deuelez wyse." (2192). This superstitious depiction is further enhanced: "Þis is a chapel of meschaunce, Þat chekke hit bytyde!" (2195) The terms 'devilish', 'mischance' and 'bad luck' create a mysterious and dangerous atmosphere. This atmosphere is highlighted by describing the seclusion and isolation of the place: "Here ar no renkes vs to rydde, rele as vus likez." (2246) This description of the area around the Green Chapel emphasizes Gawain's danger. The reader learns primarily Gawain's perspective and is faced with his fears (cf. Morgan 23). But through Gawain's viewpoint one sees the power and superiority of the Green Knight. *Sword of the Valiant* offers only little to the description of the Green Chapel. The chapel is set between a mountain inside a cave surrounded by fog (cf. Weeks 1:30:38). Furthermore, the dwelling itself does not look ugly as in the poem, but rather comfortable with green grass and trees that look like decoration, and even a servant is present (cf. 1:30:59 ff.). Hence, one does only learn little about the Green Chapel in the movie, but it is still visibly another depiction and appears less dangerous and mysterious than the depiction in the poem. Nevertheless, the depiction of the Green Knight in this scene shows similarities, at least in the beginning.

In both depictions the Green Knight appears powerful and superior in the beginning. The movie portrays the Green Knight at his reencounter with Gawain through a low angle shot (cf. Appendix – Image 1), and thus conveys "confidence, power, and control" (Mercado 9). The poem does the same by saying that the Green Knight speaks loudly and strongly (cf. 2212). Furthermore, the poem describes how the Green Knight leans on his axe: "The haÞel heldet hym fro, and on his ax rested, / Sette Þe schaft vpon schore, and to Þe scharp lened." (2331 f.) As the importance of the axe was stated earlier in this paper, the prominence of the property in this scene is still of importance. The axe is the tool of the beheading and as the Green Knight is resting on this toll, he is holding the power (cf. Walls 13). Overall, the Green Knight is powerful and dangerous in both versions. Nevertheless, this changes differently in both versions as the ending of the plot approaches.

The movie sticks to the depiction of the Green Knight being dangerous and ultimately the villain. Here, he only strikes two blows, and after missing the second one, he is attacked by Gawain and put to death. Gawain strikes him at his bare chest. Therefore, his obvious weak point, the whole in his armour, leads him to his ending after all. Furthermore, his magical green colour vanishes as he dies, he dissolves in ashes and is blown away by the wind. Hence, the Green Knight is not a human being, but still a magical creature, as he leaves no corpse. Other than that, the story ends as the villain is now defeated. The poem contrasts this depiction in every matter.

The Green Knight runs through a character change in the last scenes in the Green Chapel. After he strikes the three blows, his tone changes. He is no longer loud and dangerous but speaks: "Þenn he melez muryly with a much steuen, / And with a rynkande rurde he to Þe renk sayde." (2336 f.) As the Green Knight's tone changes after the blows, he also becomes fond of Gawain (cf. Morgan 29). Furthermore, Gawain thanks the Green Knight in the end (cf. 2408) and they embrace and kiss each other (cf. 2472). Through this change of behaviour and tone the reader can see his "compassionate recognition of the fact of human imperfection." (Shedd 10) As the Green Knight is compassionate it is difficult to see him as a villain. Also, his magical appearance is lost, as he talks to Gawain "simply as one enlightened human being" (Shedd 10) to another human being. Overall, the Green Knight appears as a sympathetic and wise human being in the chapel (cf. Shedd 11) which contrasts his first depiction. Therefore, one can say, he is not considered the dangerous villain anymore. Nevertheless, the magical elements are still demonstrated and prominent. The Green Knight being Bertilak strengthens the magical and supernatural atmosphere of the poem. Shapeshifting, as well as the survival of a beheading are incidents that cannot be explained rationally and are therefore belonging to the supernatural (Cooper 289). Thus, the Green Knight may be uncovered as not being the villain, but magic is still omnipresent. Altogether, there are differences of the depiction of the Green Knight throughout the whole plot. These differences gather especially in the ending of both versions and result in different outcomes and character developments.

4. Conclusion

There do exist differences in the portrayal of the Green Knight from beginning on. The Green Knight's outer appearance is altered in the movie in many ways. He is not as prominently green as in the poem, and not as tall and massive. The poem's Green Knight manages to intimidate only through his stature, whereas the movie's Green Knight appears to be an ordinary man dressed in green clothes. The magic of the knight which the reader can see in the poem is not visible on screen, at least in the physical appearance of the character. Furthermore, the poem introduces a profound character who can be analysed in various ways, as the example of the holly branch and the axe demonstrated. Always in contrasts stands the movie that lacks these elements. Moreover, the atmosphere around the Green Knight strengthens the different depictions of the Green Knight.

The poem offers a well-grounded atmosphere in both discussed scenes. The Green Knight's effects on the court and Gawain are reasonably described and offer an interpretation of the Green Knight acting courteously, powerful, and superior. This is depicted through his behaviour and clear magical elements. Conversely, the movie keeps its inconsistent and does not depict a strong character. Although there are aspects which describe the Green Knight's power and dominance, there are at least the same number of contradictions, like the different angles and unsuitable comical elements. This culminates in the ending of the story. The poem offers a well-structured and thorough character development, whereas the movie simply kills the Green Knight.

Overall, vulnerability is described in the movie quite obviously: a hole in the Green Knight's armour. This hole is not only symbolically but is literally his vulnerable point and reason of death. The poem portrays vulnerability in a more subtle way. First, the Green Knight misleads Gawain by demonstrating his bare neck as his weak point, which then turns out to not be the case. The Green Knight can be considered vulnerable as a whole, as he is acting as a puppet and has real no agency as he is acting out a plan that is not his own. As it comes to magic, both versions do represent magic and magical elements.

To conclude, the analysis of *Sword of the Valiant* resulted in being more difficult. Due to its volatile and inconsistent nature it is difficult to interpret individual aspects. All in all, one can say that the movie does not show "much allegiance to the original." (Williams 389)

Bibliography

Primary Literature

Tolkien, J. R. R., and E. V. Gordon. *Sir Gawain and the Green Knight*. Oxford University Press, 1967.

Weeks, Stephen, director. *Camelot: Der Fluch des goldenen Schwertes (Sword of the Valiant: The Legend of Sir Gawain and the Green Knight)*. Koch Media GmbH, 2012.

Secondary Literature

Beauregard, David N. "Moral theology in Sir Gawain and the Green Knight: the pentangle, the Green Knight, and the perfection of virtue." *Renascence*, vol. 65, no. 3, Spring 2013, pp. 146-163.

Blanch, Robert J., and Julian N. Wasserman. "The Absence of Internal Tension in "Sword of the Valiant" and "First Knight"." *Arthuriana*, vol. 10, no. 4, Winter 2000, pp. 15-32.

Brewer, Derek. "The Colour Green." *A Companion to the Gawain-Poet*, edited by Derek Brewer and Jonathan Gibson. D. S. Brewer, 1997, pp. 181-190.

Cooper, Helen. "The Supernatural." *A Companion to the Gawain-Poet*, edited by Derek Brewer and Jonathan Gibson. D. S. Brewer, 1997, pp. 277-291.

Mercado, Gustavo. *The Filmmaker's Eye: Learning (and Breaking) the Rules of Cinematic Composition.* Routledge, 2017.

Lacy, Michael. "Armour I." *A Companion to the Gawain-Poet*, edited by Derek Brewer and Jonathan Gibson. D. S. Brewer, 1997, pp. 165-173.

Mann, Jill. *Life in Words: Essays on Chaucer, the Gawain-Poet, and Malory.* University of Toronto Press, 2014.

Martin, Carl Grey. "The Cipher of Chivalry: Violence as Courtly Play in the World of Sir Gawain and the Green Knight." *The Chaucer review*, vol. 43, no. 3, Jan. 2009, pp. 311-329.

Morgan, Gerald. *The Shaping of English Poetry. Essays on Sir Gawain and the Green Knight, Langland, Chaucer and Spenser.* Peter Lang, 2010.

Pons-Sanz, Sara M. "Speech Representation as a Narrative Technique in Sir Gawain and the Green Knight." *The Review of English Studies*, vol. 70, no. 294, Apr. 2019, pp. 209-230.

Puhvel, Martin. "Sir Gawain's circling of the Green Chapel." *English language notes*, vol. 17, no. 1, Sept. 1979, pp. 10-15.

Sharma, Manish. "Hiding the harm: Revisionism and marvel in 'Sir Gawain and the Green Knight'." Papers on language & literature, vol. 44, no. 2, March 2008, pp. 168-193.

Shedd, Gordon M. "Knight in Tarnished Armour: The Meaning of "Sir Gawain and the Green Knight"." *The Modern Language Review*, vol. 62, no. 1, Jan. 1967, pp. 3-13.

Walls, Kathryn. "The Axe in Sir Gawain and the Green Knight." *ANQ*, vol. 16, no. 1, Jan. 2003, pp. 13-18.

White, Robert B. Jr. "A Note on the Green Knight's Red Eyes (GGK, 304)." *English language notes*, vol. 2, no. 4, June 1965, pp. 250-252.

Williams, David J. "Sir Gawain in Films." *A Companion to the Gawain-Poet*, edited by Derek Brewer and Jonathan Gibson. D. S. Brewer, 1997, pp. 386-392.

Appendix

Image 1: The Green Knight sitting on a horse in daylight (cf. Weeks 1:29:41).

Image 2: The Green Knight holding his axe (cf. Weeks 0:06:49).